I0201795

I Am_Unique_Rose
by Unique Rose

Copyright ©2021 by Unique Rose. All rights reserved. No portion of this book may be reproduced, stored in a retrieval system, or transmitted by any means, mechanical, electronic, photocopying, recording, or otherwise—without the prior written permission of the author.

ISBN: 978-1-7349439-6-2 Library of Congress Cataloging-in-Publication Date is available.

Project Specialist/Author Coach
Barlow Enterprises, LLC
Write Your Book Now!
Call or Text the BE Aspiring Authors Program at 478-227-5692

Legal Disclaimer
While none of the stories in this book are fabricated, some of the names and details may have been changed to protect the privacy of the individuals mentioned. Although the author and publisher have made every effort to ensure that the information in this book was correct at time of press, the author and publisher do not assume and hereby disclaim any liability to any party for any loss, damage, or disruption caused by errors or omissions, whether such errors or omissions result from negligence, accident, or any other cause.

Ordering Information
I Am_Unique_Rose may be purchased in large quantities at a discount for educational, business, or sales promotional use. For more information or to request Unique Rose as the speaker at your next event email: iamuniquerosetheauthor@gmail.com

I know the plans I have for you, declares the Lord, plans to prosper you and not to harm you, plans to give you hope and a future.

— *JEREMIAH 29:11*

DEDICATION

I dedicate this book to women who find themselves struggling with rejection, insecurities, addictions, and depression.

My story was written to inspire you not to give up on yourself. Like so many women, you may have endured trauma in your past. Despite that trauma, this book is a testament that no matter how traumatic your past was, there is still hope.

Always remember that there are no restrictions in life except those we impose upon ourselves. Our past does not define who we are or who we can become.

I hope that as you read my story, it encourages you to take the necessary steps to achieve the inner peace that you deserve.

ACKNOWLEDGEMENTS

I thank God for giving me a second chance at life. The fact that I am alive is a clear reminder of how extremely fortunate I am.

Secondly, I would like to thank my spiritual mentor, Ms. Wangui, whose words of encouragement have inspired me to never give up on God. It was because of your motivation that I was able to continue to write my story. Your sermons have uplifted others like me who struggle with doubt, weariness, and insecurity to continue to push forward on their faith journey with Christ. I pray that God continues to bless you, as you are a blessing to so many.

Lastly, I would like to thank my mother, my twin sister Rochelle Parchment, and my best friend Tawanda Moore for always being my confidant and my friend throughout this journey called life.

CONTENTS

I Am_Unique_Rose
by Unique Rose

CHAPTER 1
I DON'T BELONG HERE

Dear Diary,

Where am I, and how did I get here? I asked myself that question several times, but by the time I was able to fully grasp what was going on around me, EMTs were rolling me down a narrow white hallway. My body just lay there, lifeless. My mind repeatedly replayed the incidents in my head. I kept trying to figure it out. What could have possibly led me here? Hours passed by, but still, I had no answers. Nothing was logical. My motionless body was tightly strapped onto the worn-out stretcher in the narrow white hallway and I was lying there as if I were frozen and numb to my reality. I lay there in silence. Truthfully, I couldn't even tell you what series of events landed me in Horsham Clinic.

All I knew was that I wasn't crazy, and that I didn't belong there.

Eventually, they untied me and took me off the stretcher. I stood there, frightened, as I waited impatiently for someone to check me in. Honestly, I didn't know what to expect. I didn't know what was behind the doors of that eerie room, but what I did know was that strange, loud sounds were coming from the room next to me, and I was terrified. The walls in the hospital were paper thin, so I could hear the patients' voices as their desperate screams and moans traveled through the hallways and into the room where I was.

I even heard uncontrollable laughter and cries of help, and it all tormented me as I waited to see what was going to happen to me. I was silent, alone, and afraid.

Once they finally checked me in, they confiscated all of my property. I was not allowed to have anything. In total shock, I walked through the hallways as the residential advisors led me to my room. I couldn't believe my eyes. Never in a million years would I have imagined that I would be sitting in a mental institution . . . But I was.

Once I reached the room they assigned me, I walked in and sat on my bed. In less than five minutes, I burst into tears. I wished that this was all just another bad dream or that I could blame this surreal circumstance on some type of generational curse, but this was all my fault.

I had gone through so much in my life. I had made so many bad choices. In my constant chase for the unknown, I had disregarded my feelings and beliefs and, in the end, I had tested my faith to its limits. Despite all of that, I was still absolutely positive that the Horsham Clinic, a behavioral and psychiatric health facility, was not the place for me.

The lights in the room flickered on and off all night, which made it extremely hard to get any sleep. Not to mention that the residential advisor did rounds every twenty minutes.

Around midnight, the hospital was dead silent. I got up and headed to the bathroom to wash my face. I gazed into the mirror and saw that my eyes were bloodshot, but what scared me the most was the vacant look in my eyes. The way I looked was a clear reminder that somewhere along my journey, I had lost myself. I did not recognize the girl who looked back at me. I had given so much of myself away to people who never mattered. I had invested time that I could never get back and now, the me I knew was gone.

If I was ever going to make it out of there, I knew I had to start from the beginning.

Sincerely,
Unique Rose

CHAPTER 2
I CAN'T SLEEP

Today, I woke up feeling exhausted. My body is numb. It's really no different from any other day, honestly. The house is cold. It's always cold come winter, and for some strange reason, the heat never works on the third floor. Usually, after my mother gets done paying all the bills, there is hardly any money left from her check. She cannot afford a professional electrician. So, come winter, I pile a bunch of clothes on my bed to stay warm.

For some strange reason, that particular night, I could not fall asleep. I lay in bed for several hours, shivering, tossing and turning throughout the night and trying to stay warm. Hours went by, and I finally gave up on trying to get some sleep. I just lay in bed, staring through the window in my room and watching the traffic go by. Eventually, I managed to close my eyes, and for a quick second, I imagined myself happy, embracing my flaws, and free from bondage and self-hatred. Suddenly, I felt a cold draft of air hitting my body, causing me to feel a sense of unease, and my eyes quickly opened. At that point, I just stared at the ceiling and wondered if my circumstances would ever change.

When I was younger, I'd had so many high expectations about the way my life would turn out. I used to tell myself that one day, things would get better, but when I did not see things progressing the way I expected them to, I often found myself drifting into a dark place. That taught me, at a young age, to stop expecting so much out of life. When I was younger, I recall the many times that I sat on the bench in the school's cafeteria and ate lunch by myself while the other kids sat together. They were always laughing and sharing their memorable childhood experiences, but I sat alone. I could never relate to their stories. My childhood, as I recall it, was nothing more than an empty chapter in my life—one that I buried a long time ago. So I always tried to avoid conversations that involved reminiscing about the past.

I didn't know when I got to the point in my life when I despised who I was, but that night, no matter how hard I tried, I could not stop reflecting on my past. Thoughts of my mother ran through my mind. My mother was a single parent raising five children. I thought about how hard it must have been for her to struggle to raise her five children on her own. I wondered how she must have felt after working every day and barely having enough money to be able to put food on the table after she paid all the bills.

Then I thought about my father. He was absent from my siblings' and my life. My father was the ultimate definition of a deadbeat. He only lived twenty minutes away from us, and somehow, he never managed to come visit. Whenever I dwelt on my father, or whenever someone even brought up his name, my hatred for him somehow reappeared. I suppose it never left. The only thing that my father was consistent about was getting high, hanging out with his drunk friends, and having babies he didn't support, all of which seemed to be more important to him than raising his own children.

The more I lay there shivering, the more frustrated I became about my circumstances. I thought about how my father had robbed me of my childhood and imagined how happy my life could have been if he was a part of it. I thought about my other siblings, who were growing up without a father, without a happy childhood, and wondered if they were lonely, angry, and afraid, just like me.

There was no need for me to try to convince myself that my father cared about me, and that maybe he would rescue me. I knew he was incapable of loving anyone other than himself. He wasn't shit, and the fact that he walked away from his responsibilities said it all.

The whole night, my mind raced back and forth. All I could do was lay there, shivering. My mind slipped back into a dark place. My eyes began to water up and once again, I felt powerless. As usual, I could not help but overthink all of this. The more I thought about my circumstances, the more depressed I became. I was alone, and quite frankly, there was no need for me to fight my emotions any longer. Holding it in only made me become more angry and bitter.

So I let go of my tears, because the only thing they represented was the hurt that I felt and the guilt that I carried in my heart. It made me even more sad that the people around me could see my pain but did not bother to acknowledge it. Once I finally allowed myself to let go, tears immediately started rushing down my face. Allowing myself to let go was a relief. I was alone, and I could be myself without anyone judging me.

The longer I lay there, the more helpless I felt. At some point, I started to question my own existence. I started asking God, "Why me? What did I do to deserve to suffer like this?" But I heard nothing. For hours and hours, I heard nothing but the sound of cars driving down the street. I lay there, waiting for God to give me some type of answer that would help me understand the things that were transpiring in my life. Still, there was not a sound. I was confused and somewhat disappointed. I didn't quite know what to expect out of life. I wiped my tears and closed my eyes.

I knew the fact that I hated my father was wrong, but I also knew the things that I had gone through could have been avoided if he would have made an effort to be a part of my life. As I continued to stare at the ceiling in my room, I thought a lot about my mother, too. I'd started to resent her. I didn't quite understand why I felt that way, but I noticed that I'd started to become distant with her. I know now that it doesn't make sense, but at the time I felt that by resenting her, I was holding her accountable for my father's absence. That night, I promised myself that I would never become the woman she was. I loved my mother. Despite our struggles, she always made sure that we had food on our table and clothes on our backs, and yes, she was a young, single mother of five children who somehow managed to raise us in the suburbs, but I could never look past the fact that she was still a "struggle mother."

There were times my mother came home crying because her knee was swollen. She was in pain and frustrated because she had worked sixteen-hour shifts only to barely have enough money to put gas in her car after she paid the bills. The fact that my mother always struggled, and that we always lacked something as kids, was a sign of weakness to me. That night, I convinced myself that I was not going to be like my mother in that way. That wasn't going to be the life I was going to live. I guess you can say that after that night, my whole life changed.

It's so funny now, years later, that I can look back on my life's journey and see some of the stupid mistakes I made. I see how selfish and judgmental I was. Looking back now, I know God was with me when I tried to self-destruct. I used to try to drink myself to death because I felt like no one loved me. I attempted suicide three times. Who would have guessed that my perception of what a woman should be and my attempt to live up to that vision would eventually leave me more scarred than I was before?

All I can do when I look back at my past now is laugh. Lord knows that I am grateful that He saved me. When I was younger, my grandmother would always say that God had a funny way of making you understand things from a different perspective. Unfortunately, that typically happens through very tough life experiences. As children, we are too stubborn to listen and too young to understand. I definitely learned about life the hard way.

Months passed, and my attitude changed for the worse. I started telling myself that I was grown. Eventually, I stopped listening to what my mother said. I stopped perceiving her as a strong woman, and I stopped respecting her as one, too. I started staying up all hours of the night talking to my girlfriends. I don't know why, but for some weird reason, I felt as if I could only confide in them about my life. Our conversations were always the same. We talked about our life struggles and how neglected we felt, but mainly we discussed the lack of love we felt we received from our parents. My mother was never really an affectionate person. Because my mother never expressed her emotion for me, at a young age, I assumed that she didn't love me.

My late-night conversations with my girlfriends became the norm. I guess you can say that our pain was the bond that connected us. It was like our wounds made us closer, in some strange way. About two years after I started to disregard my mother and do anything that I wanted to do, I stopped going to school. When I was sixteen years old, I dropped out.

CHAPTER 3
DISCOVERING ROSE

You want to make God laugh? Tell Him your plans. When I was sixteen years old, I felt like I was in my prime. I was beautiful, slim, and slick with my mouth. I always hung around older people, so running games for me was easy. The fact that I was beautiful made it even easier for me to get whatever I wanted. The funny thing about life, though, is that it waits for no one. Oftentimes, as we start to mature, we look back and regret some of the choices we made as a child. The sad part about that is that by the time you realize your mistakes, there's no time for do-overs.

Dropping out of school was one of the first choices that I regretted.

I vividly remember not having to pretend anymore that I accidentally woke up late for school. In Philadelphia, you could stop attending school without being locked up for truancy at age sixteen. I happened to attend Martin Luther King High School. I felt like I wasn't learning anything, but to be quite honest, I never really applied myself. Nonetheless, when I met the age requirement, I finally stopped lying to my mother about my attendance and just stopped going to school. I told my mother the truth about a week after I dropped out of school. My mother was upset, but she knew there was nothing she could do. I was out of control. At that point in my life, I had no plans, no job, nothing. I was clueless.

Around the time that I stopped going to school, I met Tommy. Back then, I thought he was the love of my life, but time can change anything. Tommy was tall, dark, and down to earth, just the way I liked them. He was from North Philly. He was a hustler and a gentleman. You know, the type of guy you can't take home to your mother, but who you don't care to take home anyway. Yeah, he was one of those. Tommy was twenty-five and I was sixteen. His mother was on drugs most of his childhood, and his father was never around. I can admit now that was just another relationship that I built on dysfunction. It was also just another reason why our relationship could never have lasted. Even though, back then, our connection seemed so real, I know now that Tommy was just another distraction that the devil used to mislead me even more.

At a young age, Tommy was forced to assume responsibilities that made him level up. He took care of his brother and sister and attended the Community College of Philadelphia. He only lived three blocks away from me. So, when he wasn't at school or hustling, he would come pick me up and we would chill. Around that time, I became sexually active. This became another issue that my mother and I constantly fought about. Eventually, I moved out of my mom's house and moved in with my uncle and my two cousins. My cousins were both lay-backs. As long as you didn't cross their boundaries, things were cool. I loved it over there. My uncle had no rules, and loved me. Despite my flaws, he really "loved me." There was nothing that I could ask for that he wouldn't do for me. We connected on so many levels. He was like a father to me, and even though he had his flaws too, in my eyes, he was perfect.

Tommy picked me up from my uncle's house a few nights out of the week. I was able to spend the night out, so I spend most nights with him. We hit it off quickly. Sex with him was amazing. That seemed to be my only focus at that time. I was a mess. I could barely read or write, let alone fill out a job application, and still I refused to go back to school. My only priority at that time was finding happiness, and I thought that happiness could only be found by being in love with someone.

But at the age of sixteen, I knew nothing about life. I had no clue what the real definition of love was. I barely knew myself. At that age, I had no clue about my worth. I did not begin to understand the enormous value of my life until I found God years later. And even now, at the age of twenty-nine, God is still helping me to fully uncover that mystery. Back then, life was meaningless to me. To make matters worse, the more I searched and fought for love in my past relationship, the more insecure and unfulfilled I would end up feeling. Even though I physically had a partner, I still felt lonely. Mentally, spiritually, and emotionally, I was empty.

I never felt real love. Most of the men I dated only tolerated me. There was never any real appreciation, no time spent, no compassion. I always felt like I had to compromise who I was to accommodate who I was with.

Looking back, I'm not sure what I expected from those relationships. Those men were just as broken as I was. As a result, much of my young adult life was spent living with depression, because of my multiple failed relationships. Never feeling good enough kept me worried and stressed out, which only led me to look for other alternatives to ease or take away some of the pain that I had dealt with for so many years.

When I reflect on my past, I see now that it wasn't my hater, or the devil, or my so-called frenemies, that made me experience the trials and tribulations that I had gone through in life. It was me. As a matter of fact, the moment I was able to admit my faults and take accountability for my actions, God was able to help me find peace within.

Sometimes, we are our worst enemy. I agonized over the fact that I was nothing more than a sex object to men who I really wanted to love and care for me. Deep down inside, I knew that was the truth, but I wanted their affection so badly that I did anything to receive it. I don't know exactly when I lost myself, but at some point, I changed. I went from wanting love to becoming "Rose," and she was nothing more than a fantasy. I turned to alcohol to help me escape my reality, but all that drinking did was put me right back into a vulnerable state. The drinking never helped, because the feelings I had after getting drunk were never real. All that drinking ever did was make it easier for me to go out there and try to find the same things I was running from. It only left me running right back into the arms of another man, in the hope that my experience with him would be something different, something other than lies, something more than just temporary comfort.

CHAPTER 4
AT A LOSS FOR WORDS

Dear Diary,

The last couple of days have been extremely hard for me. I haven't eaten in days. Most nights, I can hardly sleep. Lately, I have found myself staying up late, staring out of my window and replaying the incidents that led me here, to Horsham Clinic. Reflecting upon my childhood has made me realize that there are a series of issues that contributed to my being here, and that those issues matter at least as much as the events that recently transpired.

Shockingly, things are starting to become so much more apparent. Being here has made me realize that there was *always* something wrong. I just never knew that what was wrong was me. At this point, it would be easy to lie and say whatever they want to hear. Quite frankly, their opinion about me doesn't matter anyway; but at some point, I needed to be honest with myself. If I'm going to have any chance of making it out of here so I can see my family again, I need to overcome the demons of my childhood.

In so many people's eyes, my life appeared perfect, but behind closed doors, I have always struggled with insecurity, addiction, and self-hate. I wanted to tenaciously conquer those battles and come out victorious. I needed to break every soul tie. So, I decided that rushing out of this institution would only give me another reason to ignore or excuse my dysfunction. I need to deal with my past and let go of everything that has hindered me.

God doesn't make mistakes.

If I give up, let go, and stop fighting now, there is a chance that I will never discover who I was meant to become. I know that the pain I have endured served a purpose. The moment I stopped and started to embrace the truth was the moment I realized that the scars I carried were never meant to make me hate myself, become bitter, or live with regret. Instead, they were meant to guide me into a space of reflection, self-growth, beauty, and wisdom. I can never go back and change my past; some things are beyond my control. I never asked for this life, but this is me, and right now, God is teaching me the true meaning of self-love. He has given me beauty for ashes, and in the midst of those ashes, I will rediscover me.

Sincerely,
Unique Rose

CHAPTER 5
REFLECTIONS

A whole year went by and it finally felt as if things were looking up for me. Just a year earlier, I'd felt like giving up on life. Now I was happy, growing in faith, and loving myself. I knew the credit only belonged to God. "Won't He do it like He said he would!" Like the old folks used to say, "Trouble don't last always." Trust the processes.

I even managed to get myself a job. I started working at the Philadelphia Nursing Home. Yes, things finally seemed to be looking up for me. You couldn't tell me nothing. I mean, my hair was getting longer, my skin was getting clearer, and I even managed to put on a couple of pounds. I made it my mission to start praying every day. The Sundays that I did not have to work were dedicated to God, so that was when I went to church. I was so grateful for what God was doing in my life and for how far He had brought me. I guess it's true that time heals everything. My smile proved that.

On my days off I would spend time at my mother's house with my twin sister, Rochelle, and my best friends, CJ and Erin. My twin sister was the total opposite of me. She was confident, smart, and patient. I tended to lack some of those traits because the path I chose as a child left me with many insecurities. My twin had a wonderful personality. I would always joke and say she was my better half, but she really was. She kept me grounded. She had a different outlook on life. I personally believed that people gravitated toward her because she was a patient person. She would always give people the benefit of the doubt. She never looked at situations from a negative perspective, and that took her farther in life. On the other hand, I always felt that trust needed to be earned, not given, because I didn't want to end up hurt again. I had put my trust in many people, only to end up demoralized. Eventually, I stopped doubting myself. I hated the feeling of discomfort that I felt after a person walked out of my life. That feeling that leaves you without dignity, self-control, and self-worth wasn't something that I wanted to ever experience again.

Through all of the disappointments I endured, I learned to trust my intuition. I stopped allowing people to get close to me. That was my way of taking control over who hurt me. It was extremely hard for me to begin trusting people again. For years, I looked at people through the same hypercritical lens that I used to view my father through. Having that type of mindset only left me limited when it came to personal growth, but I didn't care. I felt safe. I was finally happy, and that was all that mattered to me.

It took time, but I will never forget the day when I woke up feeling refreshed, motivated, and brand new. I jumped out of bed, walked to the dresser in my room, looked in the mirror, and said to myself, "You are beautiful. You are a queen, and if no one told you they love you today, God loves you!" I know it sounds silly saying it out loud, but it became a practice of mine to dedicate some time each day to allowing myself to receive some self-love and to give God thanks. I've learned through personal experiences that if you did not love yourself, no one will. My daily devotions and affirmations are therapeutic for me. I began listening to inspirational sermons. As a matter of fact, listening to TD Jakes and Joyce Myers became a major part of my morning and night routines. Twice a day, I would listen to them preach God's word. Not only were their words feeding me spiritually, but listening to them was helping me regain control over my life. I finally felt safe. I finally felt free.

The feelings of shame, guilt, and hurt that I'd once carried with me slowly started to disappear. I was gaining strength. I was building a relationship with God, and through that relationship, God was giving me contentment. Knowing that God loved me and never looked at me as a failure, despite my mistakes, gave me the strength I needed to keep going. I knew God had a purpose for my life, and that led me to continue to walk in faith.

CHAPTER 6
WHAT'S NEXT?

Months went by and I continued to keep myself busy by working. Working was the only thing that kept Tommy off my mind. The more and more I worked, the less I thought about him. Eventually, our relationship started to die down.

I managed to blend in at work for quite some time. I separated myself from the crowd, but eventually that only made people more curious about me. I started making friends at work about six months in. When I met Keisha, our work relationship quickly blossomed into a real friendship outside of work. When we were not at work cracking on people, we would occasionally hang out at her house, drinking. We didn't make much money at work, so we couldn't really afford to do anything extravagant, but that never stopped us from having fun. We would talk about the people at our job that we couldn't stand. We also talked about fashion and music, but mainly we talked about boys.

Keshia was dating a guy named John, who happened to be twenty-seven years old. Keshia was only twenty-two, but she was mature for her age and she had a good heart. We became close very fast, because I felt like I could trust her. When I was with her, I felt safe. I didn't know what it was about her, but she was definitely different from the females that I'd met in my past. Truth be told, she wasn't grimy. She didn't have much, but she was content. I could tell that she was a genuine person. I never had to second-guess her motives. She was not one of those girls who only befriended you, scheming just to find out your business. No. Not Keshia. She was different.

After about eight months of hanging out with her, I noticed that she had been having issues in her relationship. At that time, it had been months since I had heard from Tommy. I thought he had found someone new, and that was the reason he'd stopped hitting me up, but I was wrong. Shortly after wondering why I had not heard from him in so long, I found out through a friend of his that he had been locked up on drug charges. Me and Tommy's relationship had been fading for quite a while, so it didn't really bother me that he was locked up, and as selfish as it sounds, I was too busy finally loving myself to care about anyone else. So when I heard the news that he was locked up, I didn't really feel any type of way. Even though I loved him, we were never official. When I found out he was doing him, I quickly stopped caring and started doing me.

A couple weeks after I found out that Tommy was locked up, I found out that Keshia had finally broken up with her lying, cheating, trifling boyfriend. I was so happy for her. He didn't respect or appreciate her worth, so when she finally came to her senses and said she was through with him, I made sure I threw my girl a celebration! That Friday, me and Keshia got dressed and ended up pre-gamed at my mother's house before we went out. I ended up taking her out to a bar down on Twenty-Second Street in North Philly that night. We go so lit. I could tell she was enjoying herself. It was a relief to see her smiling and stress-free again, but seeing her happy was a clear reminder of how unhappy I was. I knew right then and there that it was time for me to move on and start dating again.

CHAPTER 7
LOVE IS BLIND

Dear Diary,

Who would have known that behind these shattered walls lay so much beauty?

Lord, it is amazing how much peace You have given me. There were many moments in my life when I thought I would lose my mind, and even now, with the circumstance of being thrown into a place like this, forgotten and labeled as crazy, You still continue to give me hope by speaking life into my situation.

Lord, Your words allowed me to tune out the negative emotions that I feel toward myself and the misconceptions that others have about me. I know that their opinions about me do not change the plans that you have set for my life. Looking back over the years, I know that those seeds of doubt that were planting in my mind were from the enemy. I was never powerless, but I did allow my anger and insecurity to discourage and draw me away from you, Lord. I settled for less every time I believed the lies of the enemy. I let my pain linger and bleed into my relationships. I'm not proud of that, today. I made a lot of poor decisions when it came to friendships and companionship. I chose people who honestly did not have my best interest at heart. Trauma was the only thing we shared, and because I held on to that broken bond, I unconsciously encountered the same obstacles year after year. In the end, I hindered my progress and was kept stagnant.

God, You know that I'm far from perfect, and as bad as it may sound, I went into a lot of those relationships knowing they were no good for me. As hard as it is to stomach the truth, my truth needs to be told. I'm hoping that when it's all said and done, I can stop reliving my past. It's been said that "You're only as sick as the secrets you keep, "and the truth is that in my last relationship with a man name Russ, I endured so much torture just to be with someone who I knew really didn't love me. I expected loyalty from a man I knew couldn't even be honest with me. The last two years, I stayed in denial because it was hard for me to accept the truth that the relationship was over. It's sad to say that the only attention I received from a man that I loved and gave my mind, body, and soul to was in the form of affliction, abuse, and manipulation. That wasn't love. Who knew that you could love someone so much that you lost yourself in the process? Well, I did it, and as foolish as it sounds, I loved someone that continued to hurt me. Yet, I stayed.

I stayed hoping that one day, he would realize how much I had sacrificed to be with him, but he never did. Nothing ever changed. I just endured more pain and ended up wasting six years of my life with a man who gave me nothing to show for it. Nothing. Nothing more than embarrassment. I tried to revive something that had died a long time ago. I replayed his lies in my head over and over again. I fed myself false hope and ended up breaking my own heart in the process. The nerve of me, to think that I could change a man, and a narcissistic man, at that. What I failed to realize was that what I value determines my worth. I valued someone who didn't respect or love me, and that was never what God intended for me.

Sincerely,
Unique Rose

CHAPTER 8
DEATH BRINGS MEANING TO LIFE

A long time ago, I remember listening to a pastor preach a sermon about the suffering and misfortunes he had endured as a young man. He talked about his many setbacks and the trials he had encountered throughout his life. For as long as he could remember, he had been an addict. For years, he was living on the streets, addicted, homeless, and hopeless. Until one day when he heard a pastor preach a sermon about God that ultimately changed his life. Not long after that, he became a believer. He stopped using drugs and was eventually able to clean himself up, but it wasn't until he had gotten clean that he was able to see the meaning of his life. He knew that when he accepted Jesus Christ as his personal savior, his whole life changed. He started preaching all around the world, sharing his personal testimony in the hope that he would be able to save someone else's life.

"Death brings meaning to life."

The pastor explained that this was a quote that he lived by. He believed that when his carnal lifestyle died, he was able to discover God's purpose for his life. Years later, I had that quote tattooed on my body. Around that time, things in my life were going pretty good for me. Well, at least I thought they were. Actually, by the time I realized that things weren't as good as I thought, they had already begun to go downhill.

CHAPTER 9
FALLING SLOWLY

I'd started dating a man named Russ. He was an older gentleman who I had met through a mutual friend. We'd spoken a few times in passing, but it was nothing serious. At the time, I was unaware of how into me Russ really was. One day, at a party we both attended, he finally mustered up enough courage to ask me out on a date. I thought it was cute, honestly. I will admit that at first, I was very cautious. As lonely as I felt, the thought of getting hurt was a feeling that I never wanted to experience again. So I played hard to get. I kept my guard up and pretended that I was uninterested for as long as I could, but eventually, he won me over with his charm.

Russ made me feel special. He was patient and took the time to get to know me. Without a doubt, he was different. When I met Russ, I thought my prayers were answered. I thought God had blessed me with the love of my life. I thought Russ was my angel in disguise. I soon found out that he wasn't. Russ was just another lesson learned. In the beginning, everything was good. Russ and I would go out on dates every weekend and talk on the phone every day. We were inseparable. It felt amazing to finally meet someone who was really into me, but I ignored all the red flags.

Russ made me forget about everything I had ever been through in my past. He didn't pressure me into anything. I was able to take things slow with him. I waited months until I laid down with him, and when we did finally connect on a sexual level, it was unimaginable. I shared everything with him. My fears, my pain, my past, and my body, and he had never judged me. I felt safe lying next to him.

I woke up to long kisses, and Russ's scent soon became my favorite fragrance. Words cannot describe how he made me feel. I was so grateful to have him in my life. I always tried to spend any free time I had with him. Russ and I would occasionally take trips out of town together. We would go out to eat. Sometimes, we would just lay around in bed all day, watching movies. I loved being in his company. There were so many qualities that I loved about him. Russ worked long hours and he came home tired. He would always say, "I need to unwind before I go to bed." That typically involved him sitting in front of the television all night and having a drink until it was time for him to go to sleep. That was something that would always irritate me about him, but it was really his way of handling his stress.

For once in my life, I felt like I had met someone who I was able to be myself around. That little girl who always lived her life in fear, afraid of people judging her, had finally met someone who she was able to open up to. That was definitely a feeling that I had never felt before. I had never experienced that sense of security with a man. There wasn't anything that Russ wouldn't do to put a smile on my face. He made it his priority to make me happy, and anything that I wanted, he provided. I wanted that feeling to last for a lifetime, but how naive was I to think it would?

After several months, we started to learn each other's ways. Russ took the time to learn what I was interested in, but he overlooked a major weakness. As the relationship started to blossom, so did my drinking. Russ also enjoyed drinking. There wasn't a day that went by that he didn't have a drink, or two for that matter. So we would often go to the local bars together, and as time progressed, so did my drinking. I started drinking every day. Russ didn't even realize that I had an addiction. He was so infatuated with the way I looked that he never even noticed it.

I had always battled with alcoholism. I started drinking at an early age. For me, it was a learned behavior. Growing up, I watched my family model drinking excessively. As a matter of fact, it was as if being a drunk was something to be proud of in our household. It felt as if it was some type of generational curse, because I was not able to break the addiction no matter how hard I tried.

Ultimately, alcohol became my downfall. It was one of the reasons I couldn't grow spiritually, and it was why I could not embrace the changes that God was making in my life. For as long as I could remember, my life was stagnant, because I let my environment, my emotions, my self-doubt, my circumstances, and my flesh overshadow what God had prophesied for my life. I knew in my heart that I was destined to be great, but I was too small-minded and afraid to see anything other than what people saw in me.

A bottle of rum was my secret medication. I ran to rum whenever things became overwhelming for me. Throughout my life, people would always try to define me as crazy, but I wasn't crazy. I was just misunderstood. I was passionate. I carried my heart on my sleeve. I was truly just a girl who wanted love and attention and, once again, I was headed for self-destruction.

For years, while dating Russ, I was able to hide my insecurities with a smile and a bottle of rum. Even with all of my issues, I still had morals. I still stood for something, and what I loved and valued in Russ was something totally different than what he saw in me. I don't know when I accepted that truth, but I thank God that I was able to wake up from the idea of someone coming to rescue me. Somewhere down the line, I realized that I was wasting too much time and energy on what wasn't guaranteed to last forever. When I talked to Russ about settling down and having a future together, it only led to arguments. I guess that was God's way of telling me that he wasn't my soulmate after all. That should have been the moment when I ran and never looked back, but even with all the wisdom and guidance that God was providing me, I still couldn't gather enough courage to leave him. Looking back now, I think I was more afraid of leaving him and finding out that someone else had taken my place, because I made every excuse I could to justify why I stayed instead of listening to my own heart.

I stayed with Russ and forfeited my happiness, instead of walking away and just letting go. I fed myself false hope and convinced myself that he would change. It was my pattern. I drowned my emotions. I silenced my voice. I fed my void with temporary fixes, and I believed every lie he told me. I buried all my expectations, just to keep someone who didn't deserve to be kept in the first place. Still, I have no regrets. The greatest gift I ever received from Russ came from his absence, which taught me how to rely on God when I couldn't rely on Russ.

I thought that Russ and I would be together forever, but God had different plans for my life. Looking back now, I'm so thankful to God for all the setbacks and situations that caused things not to work out for us. Like the other relationships I'd been in, that experience helped shape me into the strong woman I am today.

As I started to change and grow in my faith, Russ grew cold and resentful toward me. I know now that this was never meant to break me; it was God's way of molding me. God was preparing me for something bigger than what I saw for myself. Even with all the childhood trauma that I endured, God still saw purpose, success, and purity in me. I was just too immature and selfish at that time to accept that part of my story. God never told me that my journey wouldn't be rough at times, though He did promise that He wouldn't leave me, nor forsake me. Being with Russ was an eye-opener for me. It showed me that what I was searching for could only come from within. Once I had figured that out, I made it my mission to break every chain and bond that the devil held over my life. Who would have known that those countless nights I spent lying next to Russ, crying myself to sleep, would serve a purpose? Not me, but those unpleasant nights turned out to be "no tears wasted" moments. God empowered me to transform those feelings of rejection, loneliness, and anxiety into words, so that I could tell my story and finally receive peace.

CHAPTER 10
TRUTH HURTS

Dear Diary,

How foolish was I to think that karma wouldn't catch up with me? Not only did I ignore my feelings, but I failed to acknowledge and obey God. I'll admit it: I was stubborn. Even after God exposed my imperfections, I still refused to surrender to Him and to the call He had on my life.

I remember praying for love, but I wasn't patient enough to wait for God to bring the right person into my life. Over the years, I overlooked the lies of so many men. I refused to listen to my gut when it told me time and time again, " Sis, he ain't the one for you!" I was desperate, unsure, and so busy living my life engaged in this never-ending, dead-end search to nowhere that eventually I wasn't even sure what I was looking for.

Nonetheless, I am not 100 percent surprised at how things turned out for me. I know that the only reason I am still here today in Horsham Clinic is because of the seeds I have sown.

When I started my relationship with Russ, I stopped praising God. Russ's love became my idol. In the end, I guess you could say I got exactly what I was looking for, and then some. One of the biggest regrets I have is how I compared myself to others back then. When I looked at people around me, all I could see was everything that I had ever prayed for. I saw love. I saw a family. I saw children. *When will that be me?* I wondered. The problem is, I never took the time out to consider their struggles or the tears and the sacrifices that those people had made to be in the positions they were in. All I saw were their crooked smiles. I didn't know it then, but I had a covetous spirit. My tainted desires created secret motives that only God could see.

I was mad at the world because I didn't have things that I honestly wasn't mentally prepared for, but without prayer or God in my life, how would I have known that? Once I stopped praying, that was the gateway for Satan to plant jealousy in my life. To be real, I didn't have the things I wanted because it wasn't my season to have them yet. God knew I wasn't ready yet. I needed to fully mature and come into alignment with Him first.

Thank you, Lord, for always having grace and mercy over my life and for humbling me before life did! God knew I needed to get rid of the hurt that I had let linger over the years so that my biased opinions about others could no longer block the soulmate that God had for me. I had always judged others, but words can't describe how I felt as I lay in that hospital bed. Finally, I realized what God had been saying to me all along, and I was happy to know that God was still covering me.

For many years, I focused on what I didn't have. As a result, my life was full of turmoil. I secretly envied people, and never considered that the people I envied were living a carnal lifestyle. They weren't even "saved." To know now that I risked my life and my family's life by making irresponsible decisions feels like a heavier burden than my actual sins. I pray daily that God removes this guilt from my heart, because in the end, I know there is no one else to blame but myself.

This life of mine is the work of my own hands

Sincerely,
Unique Rose

CHAPTER 11
THIS TOO SHALL PASS

Finally, he told me that he didn't love me anymore. That was when my relationship with Russ ended. God was shedding light on the things I couldn't see. God made people's true intentions toward me so clear that I could not deny what I saw and heard. Looking back at it now, God was exposing all the negative things in my life that I needed to get rid of. He was revealing my enemies, and their truths were finally coming to the light.

I tried my best to stay balanced by concealing my pain the best way I knew how, and although I knew it needed to end, Russ's absence was bittersweet for me. I knew that I deserved better, but I still had a wound that needed to mend. I felt like my life was over. Never in a million years would I have thought that someone that I loved and with whom I had shared everything would tell me he no longer loved me.

Those words triggered something in me. His rejection triggered a lot of unresolved emotions that I had when I was younger, and brought up many painful memories from my childhood. I started to recall all of the dysfunctional relationships that I was involved in prior to Russ. The whole breakup drew me back into my dark place, and back into my past. Those depressing thoughts repeatedly played in my head, and feelings of never being good enough resurfaced. Once again, I felt that I was incapable of being loved. I felt like I was at my lowest, and that I was there alone. I sank deeper and deeper into depression. I even began to question my own existence. The hurt that I endured after Russ's and my relationship ended was something that I never wanted to experience again. I felt worthless. I felt used, and I felt abandoned by someone to whom I had given my all.

On numerous nights, I told God that I would no longer be a slave to my addiction. I told God that I no longer wanted to hide behind my truth and that if everyone who came into my life was going to leave my life, then there was just no reason to live.

I just wanted to be free from everything that had kept me enslaved, but the destructive patterns that I kept repeating were God's way of telling me to let go. I never would have thought that I would try to take my own life, but I did. Thank you, Jesus, for having other plans for me! God saved my life.

CHAPTER 12
TRANSITIONING

Dear Diary,

When I was finally given the opportunity to tell my side of the story, I did, and the psychiatrist decided to release me. Today makes it three years since I've been out, and life for me has changed dramatically.

Once I came home, I made it my mission to seek redemption by trying to make amends for my past. Even with that, God is teaching me that sometimes, in order to flourish, you may have to walk alone. I thank God every day for giving me a new perspective on life. Most of all, I thank God for forgiving me. I faced so many challenges in my past, and although I know that my past will always be a part of me, I choose not to be the person I was anymore.

Now I live life with a purpose, and that purpose is to serve God by encouraging women not to measure their value based on other people's perceptions of them, and not by their failures. I want women to know that their worth is measured by the adversities they overcome in their lives. I believe that the hardships and misfortunes I endured in my life led me to my real encounter with God.

Some afflictions are meant to become testimonies, not dilemmas. Our suffering is not meant to draw us away from God, but to bring us closer to Him so that we can experience His grace and mercy.

To be alive today is a blessing, and I thank God for giving me a second chance at life. Even in my weakest moments, God turned my insecurities, my shame, and my trauma into something so beautiful, by giving me the ability to write my story.

God always knew who I was destined to become—even when I did not.

I will never compromise my uniqueness again, because I was made to shine. After everything that I have experienced, I know that no loss compares to losing my relationship with God.

I am forever grateful.

Thank you, Jesus.

Sincerely,
Unique Rose

PRAYER OF SALVATION

DEAR LORD JESUS,

I KNOW THAT I AM A SINNER, AND I ASK
FOR YOUR FORGIVENESS.

I BELIEVE YOU DIED FOR MY SINS AND
ROSE FROM THE DEAD.

I TURN FROM MY SINS AND INVITE YOU TO
COME INTO MY HEART AND LIFE.

I WANT TO TRUST AND FOLLOW YOU AS
MY LORD AND SAVIOR.

AMEN.

ABOUT THE AUTHOR

Unique Rose is an inspired Christian author who resides in Pennsylvania, PA. She received her Associate Degree in Science from Eastern University. Her plans are to further her education in the near future. Unique Rose hopes to continue to inspire others through her books by sharing her outlook on life from a spiritual perspective.

By sharing her truth, she believes that others will be encouraged and open to learning about the goodness of God. Most importantly, she wants her work to inspire people to receive Jesus as their Lord and Savior.

Be on the lookout for her up and coming book, *Uniquely Me,* a diary for women and children, and for her free unisex journal, *Jesus is the Light.*

To learn more about Unique Rose, follow her at I Am_ Unique_Rose on Instagram.

HELPFUL RESOURCES

If you or someone you know is feeling depressed, suicidal, or anxious, or just needs help facing life's challenges, do not give up!

I have listed some churches that offer prayer-line services and on-demand sermons.

I also listed inspirational songs that you can play to lift your spirit.

NEW COVENANT CHURCH OF PHILADELPHIA

Prayer Line 515.604.9000
Access Code 605781#
Back up call 1-857-957-1149

SERMONS ON YOUTUBE

Subscribe to *NCCPHILLY*
Website https://nccop.church

THE POTTER'S TOUCH MINISTRY

Prayer Line 1.800.247.4672

SERMONS ON YOUTUBE

Subscribe to *T.D. Jakes*
Website https://www.tdjakes.org

JOYCE MEYER MINISTRIES

Prayer Line   1-866-480-1528

SERMONS ON YOUTUBE

Subscribe to Joyce Meyer, *Enjoying Everyday Life*
https://journey.joycemeyer.org

MUSIC TO UPLIFT YOUR SPIRIT

MARANDA CURTIS
"Nobody Like You Lord"
"Way Maker"

WILLIAMS MCDOWELL
"I Give Myself Away"
"Withholding Nothing"

ISABEL DAVIS
"Wide as the Sky"
"The Call"

MARVIN SAPP
"Never Would've Made It"
"The Best in Me"

TASHA COBBS
"Fill Me Up"
"Overflow"
"Break Every Chain"

HEZEKIAH WALKER
"God Favored Me"
"Grateful" (Reprise)

FRED HAMMOND
"No Weapons"
"Keeping My Mind"

YOLANDA ADAM
"Open My Heart"

TASHA COBBS LEONARD FEAT-
JIMI CRAVITY
"You Know My Name"

MICHAEL W. SMITH
"Surrounded (Fight My
Battles)"

TAMELA MANN
"Take Me to The King"

If you or someone you know is going through depression or is in crisis, please call the suicide prevention hotline at 1.800.273.TALK (8255) or text the Crisis Text Line now. Text HELLO to 741741.

Both services are free and are available twenty-four hours a day, seven days a week.

SUICIDE PREVENTION HOTLINE

Call: 1.800.273.8255
Text: HELLO to 741741
Visit: https://suicidepreventionlifeline.org

JOURNAL

"THEREFORE MY HEART IS GLAD,
AND MY GLORY REJOICES;
MY FLESH ALSO WILL REST IN HOPE."

PSALM 16:9

I AM_UNIQUE_ROSE

_____

_____

_____

_____

_____

_____

_____

_____

_____

_____

_____

_____

_____

_____

"YOU ARE MY HIDING PLACE AND MY SHIELD; I HOPE IN YOUR WORD."

PSALM 119:114

I AM_UNIQUE_ROSE

_____

_____

_____

_____

_____

_____

_____

_____

_____

_____

_____

_____

_____

_____

_____

"O ISRAEL, HOPE IN THE LORD; FOR WITH THE LORD THERE IS MERCY, AND WITH HIM IS ABUNDANT REDEMPTION."

PSALM 130:7

I AM_UNIQUE_ROSE

"THE LORD TAKES PLEASURE IN THOSE WHO FEAR HIM, IN THOSE WHO HOPE IN HIS MERCY."

PSALM 147:11

I AM_UNIQUE_ROSE

_____

_____

_____

_____

_____

_____

_____

_____

_____

_____

_____

_____

_____

_____

_____

"FOR SURELY THERE IS A HEREAFTER, AND YOUR HOPE WILL NOT BE CUT OFF."

PROVERBS 23:18

I AM_UNIQUE_ROSE

"BLESSED IS THE MAN WHO TRUSTS IN THE LORD, AND WHOSE HOPE IS THE LORD."

JEREMIAH 17:7

I AM_UNIQUE_ROSE

"'THE LORD IS MY PORTION,' SAYS MY SOUL, 'THEREFORE I HOPE IN HIM!'"

LAMENTATIONS 3:24

I AM_UNIQUE_ROSE

"THE LORD YOUR GOD IN YOUR MIDST, THE MIGHTY ONE, WILL SAVE; HE WILL REJOICE OVER YOU WITH GLADNESS, HE WILL QUIET YOU WITH HIS LOVE, HE WILL REJOICE OVER YOU WITH SINGING."

ZEPHANIAH 3:17

I AM_UNIQUE_ROSE

"HIS LORD SAID TO HIM, 'WELL DONE, GOOD AND FAITHFUL SERVANT; YOU WERE FAITHFUL OVER A FEW THINGS, I WILL MAKE YOU RULER OVER MANY THINGS. ENTER INTO THE JOY OF YOUR LORD."

MATTHEW 25:21

I AM_UNIQUE_ROSE

_____

_____

_____

_____

_____

_____

_____

_____

_____

_____

_____

_____

_____

_____

_____

"NOW HOPE DOES NOT DISAPPOINT, BECAUSE THE LOVE OF GOD HAS BEEN POURED OUT IN OUR HEARTS BY THE HOLY SPIRIT [WHICH] WAS GIVEN TO US."

ROMANS 5:5

I AM_UNIQUE_ROSE

"REJOICING IN HOPE, PATIENT IN
TRIBULATION, CONTINUING STEADFASTLY
IN PRAYER."

ROMANS 12:12

I AM_UNIQUE_ROSE

_____

_____

_____

_____

_____

_____

_____

_____

_____

_____

_____

_____

_____

_____

"NOW MAY THE GOD OF HOPE FILL YOU WITH ALL JOY AND PEACE IN BELIEVING, THAT YOU MAY ABOUND IN HOPE BY THE POWER OF THE HOLY SPIRIT."

ROMANS 15:13

I AM_UNIQUE_ROSE

"EYE HAS NOT SEEN, NOR EAR HEARD, NOR HAVE ENTERED INTO THE HEART OF MAN THE THINGS WHICH GOD HAS PREPARED FOR THOSE WHO LOVE HIM."

1 CORINTHIANS 2:9

I AM_UNIQUE_ROSE

"THE EYES OF YOUR UNDERSTANDING BEING ENLIGHTENED; THAT YOU MAY KNOW WHAT IS THE HOPE OF HIS CALLING, WHAT ARE THE RICHES OF THE GLORY OF HIS INHERITANCE IN THE SAINTS."

EPHESIANS 1:18

I AM_UNIQUE_ROSE

_____

_____

_____

_____

_____

_____

_____

_____

_____

_____

_____

_____

_____

_____

_____

"BUT LET US WHO ARE OF THE DAY BE SOBER, PUTTING ON THE BREASTPLATE OF FAITH AND LOVE, AND AS A HELMET THE HOPE OF SALVATION."

1 THESSALONIANS 5:8

I AM_UNIQUE_ROSE

"IN HOPE OF ETERNAL LIFE WHICH GOD,
WHO CANNOT LIE,
PROMISED BEFORE TIME BEGAN."

TITUS 1:2

I AM_UNIQUE_ROSE

_____

_____

_____

_____

_____

_____

_____

_____

_____

_____

_____

_____

_____

_____

_____

"AND EVERYONE WHO HAS THIS HOPE IN
HIM PURIFIES HIMSELF,
JUST AS HE IS PURE."

1 JOHN 3:3

I AM_UNIQUE_ROSE

"AND GOD WILL WIPE AWAY EVERY TEAR FROM THEIR EYES; THERE SHALL BE NO MORE DEATH, NOR SORROW, NOR CRYING. THERE SHALL BE NO MORE PAIN, FOR THE FORMER THINGS HAVE PASSED AWAY."

REVELATION 21:4

I AM_UNIQUE_ROSE

www.ingramcontent.com/pod-product-compliance
Lightning Source LLC
Chambersburg PA
CBHW061732020426
42331CB00006B/1215